Don't Hurry, Be Happy!

# don't hurry,
# be happy!

*650 smart ways to slow down
and enjoy life*

## ernie j. zelinski

Prima Publishing

© 1999 by Ernie J. Zelinski

PRIMA PUBLISHING and colophon are registered trademarks of Prima Communications, Inc.

**Library of Congress Cataloging-in-Publication Data**

Zelinski, Ernie J.
    Don't hurry, be happy! : 650 smart ways to slow down and enjoy life /
Ernie J. Zelinski.
        p.    cm.
    ISBN 0-7615-1855-X
    1. Conduct of life. I. Title.
BJ1581.2.z45 1999
158.1 dc21                                                            99-16252
                                                                          CIP

99    00    01    02    03    HH    10    9    8    7    6    5    4    3    2

Printed in the United States of America

**HOW TO ORDER**

Single copies may be ordered from Prima Publishing, P.O. Box 1260BK, Rocklin, CA 95677; telephone (916) 632-4400. Quantity discounts are also available. On your letterhead, include information concerning the intended use of the books and the number of books you wish to purchase.

**Visit us online at www.primalifestyles.com**

# Contents

133503

# Introduction

Are you hurrying more and more but feeling left behind? If you are overwhelmed by the frantic pace of the modern Western world and want to have more time to relax and think, this book is for you. The advice in this book can lead you into a more fulfilled life in and away from the office.

A recent research study at Penn State University indicated that what we perceive as a time crunch in large measure is just an erroneous perception. We all have enough time to do the important and enjoyable things, but we squander it. We must eliminate irritating distractions, energy leaks, and time wasters. The secret is to reconcile our work with our personal lives so that we work less, consume less, and enjoy life much more.

This book is actually for ambitious people and not for lazy people. It is for individuals who want to find ways to get to know themselves and others better, instead of constantly being busy with no real payoffs. Doing what the majority in society is doing doesn't take any real effort, brains, or risk. It's easy to be busy, just to be busy. It's easy to fill our lives with activities and then complain about the time crunch. It's easy to lie on the couch and watch TV for two or three hours. However, it takes guts to be different, slow down, know ourselves better, and do some real living.

Sayings—sometimes called "folk wisdom"—such as "Idle hands are the devil's workshop," "Rest makes rusty," "Labor is in itself a pleasure," and "Labor warms; sloth harms," urge us to work hard, no matter what the consequences. I think it is better to abide by proverbs and quotations such as "To work is human; to loaf divine," "No person who is in a hurry is quite civilized," and "Few women and fewer men have enough character to be idle." These support a good work/life balance—and even occasional laziness.

There is an interesting paradox you should keep in mind if you don't want to feel so hurried with your life. Contrary to public belief, speeding up and rushing around in a mad frenzy is not the way to create more time for the more important and enjoyable things. The best way to create more time in your life is to slow down. Then you can really live. Enjoy the moment, no matter what you are doing, and life won't be so hurried.

Hurry sickness results in health problems such as excessive stress, bad nerves, ticks, indigestion, high blood pressure, heart problems, and ulcers. Researchers suggest that hurry sickness can ultimately contribute to heart attacks and certain forms of cancer. Researchers have also shown that a better work/life balance relieves stress, improves moods, increases life satisfaction, and even boosts the immune system. Slowing down, getting rid of the clutter, and doing less work will allow you to pursue more meaningful things. You will enjoy life more.

I should emphasize that this book offers a whole lot of suggestions. Besides the general suggestions, one section deals specifically with money, and another deals with the workplace. Perish the thought of trying to implement all of these suggestions in your life in the next month or two. You will end up more hurried and stressed than ever.

Look for those suggestions that really appeal to you. Adopt them in your lifestyle so that you end up as the sensible—even wise—tortoise instead of the foolish hare. Ultimately you will be the winner—not those hurried people rushing ahead of you in traffic, working more hours than you, and trying to acquire more possessions than you.

Success at the office is not worth anything if you are a failure at home. The early Greeks talked about the golden mean—a balance between poverty and excess. I hope this book helps you get off the treadmill and experience the golden mean.

# Happiness 101

To create more time for enjoying that mysterious and unpredictable phenomenon called life, minimize your search for the secret to it. You don't need to fully understand life to fully enjoy it.

Accept that happiness doesn't care how you get there. Many people with limited financial resources are extremely happy in this world, and many people with lots of money are extremely unhappy. Happiness doesn't care how hard you work, how big your house is, how much you pay for your clothes, or how fancy your car is.

Pay heed to the words of Henry David Thoreau: "Oh, God, to reach the point of death and realize you have never lived at all."

When you think you don't have time to enjoy a sunset, think again. The most important moment to stop and enjoy a sunset is when you don't have time for it.

Every so often—not too often—treat yourself to something you are not supposed to have. Instead of the salad for lunch, have a big bag of gourmet potato chips with a rich dip. This is your reward for regularly eating all those healthy meals and working so diligently.

You were given three special gifts when you were born: the gifts of life, love, and laughter. Learn to share these gifts with the rest of the world, and the rest of the world will play with you.

Take an unexpected day off work and loaf it away to experience what it's like to be a member of the leisure class. Enjoy your prosperity. This day off comes compliments of me. (There's no need to mention my name to your boss.)

When was the last time you whistled a tune or sang a song? Next time you are in the shower, whistle or sing to your heart's content.

You can waste precious time taking more than a minute to make insignificant decisions such as which flavor of ice cream to buy. Flip a coin if you have a hard time making a decision. Alternatively, instead of choosing vanilla or chocolate, go for something really out of the ordinary like snake berry.

**Choose to be around people who make you laugh.**

Here is another way to make quick decisions for life's rather insignificant matters to save time: dice living. For example, number six restaurants from 1 to 6, including at least one expensive one and one in the wilder part of town that could be quite the adventure. Then roll the die, and go to the restaurant whose number matches the die.

Don't compare yourself to Martha Stewart. Your contentment with your own life will come from accepting yourself.

Don't wait for someone else to improve your life: take the initiative to light the fire instead of standing around waiting to be warmed by it.

Just as important as deciding what you want in life is deciding what you don't want. Make a list of the things you don't want. Work toward not getting them. Allow yourself to give up those things in life that don't make you happy.

It's not wise to hold off on being happy. Give this some serious consideration: The Great Creator gave you 86,400 seconds today. How many have you utilized so far to enjoy life?

The three essentials for prime real estate are location, location, and location. There are also three essentials for enjoying life to the fullest: attitude, attitude, and attitude. Develop and maintain a healthy attitude, and life will be much more fulfilling.

Read every Calvin and Hobbes cartoon book you can get your hands on.

Watch less TV and more sunsets. The average individual in the United States and Canada watches three and a half hours of TV a day. No wonder we don't have time for more pleasurable and satisfying activities.

Don't shy away from trying a new sport or activity because you feel you can't become good at it. Accept that it's worth doing even if you end up doing it badly.

Take more risks in life—at work and play. Too much safety can be dangerous.

Experience what many natives experience who never wear shoes. There's nothing like walking barefoot on the grass or in sand in the early morning and continuing on through the whole day.

Read the classic story *The Little Prince* by Antoine de Saint Exupéry to put life in proper perspective. This book will change your thinking about what is really important in life. If you have read it, read it again for more hidden truths.

Ask yourself, "Why should I slow down and really live by being more leisurely?" Make a list. Your answers should relate to benefits such as personal growth, higher self-esteem, less stress, improved health, and better family life. Some more benefits are excitement and adventure, more satisfaction from life, more happiness, and an overall higher quality of life.

Resist cultural influences and popular opinion about the benefits of work and the need for economic growth. These beliefs exhaust resources, increase pollution, and force the extinction of many plant and animal species. Growth for the sake of growth is the philosophy of cancer cells.

If you are suffering from boredom due to a midlife crisis, put your boredom at risk. Do something radically new—like moving to Thailand—so that your midlife crisis is transformed into a midlife adventure.

Keep close to your heart in work and play. Discover your mission in life and actively pursue it. Life will be less hurried.

**On a cloudy day, create your own sunshine.**

Think big this weekend. Go somewhere so that you are away from home and the office for at least two nights. Three is better.

Clean up your messy closets. It's amazing what a drain of energy a disorganized and cluttered closet can be.

Be an art critic. Visit an art gallery and focus on just one painting that you find intriguing.

To determine if you're working too hard, just ask your spouse or close friends for their opinions. Pay attention to what they have to say, and adjust your life accordingly.

Rank the following life challenges according to importance in your life: partner, kids, health, personal growth, job, community, spirituality, education. Only you can decide whether you have your priorities right and are living according to them.

Free up more time for yourself by curtailing the number of hours you spend on the Internet. Try not to surf the Web unless it is absolutely necessary or highly educational.

Don't waste precious time arguing with irrational people. Keep your cool and be on your way. Remember, if you catch yourself arguing with an idiot, he or she is doing the same thing.

Give serious consideration to the Zen philosophy that the less we need in material and physical comforts, the freer we become. We are imprisoned by the things that we are most attached to: jobs, houses, cars, egos, and so forth. Learn to let go of these things and you will be released from your prison.

Avoid the destructive habit of trying to cram "productive" activity into every minute of your life. Learn to relax on an airplane flight instead of delving into more work. Watch the other passengers. Start a conversation with the person beside you. Read a trashy novel.

After the home and office, shopping malls are the place where Americans spend the most time. This world offers myriad more interesting things to do than hanging around malls.

D o some of the things you loved doing when you were a kid:

⊚ Skip rocks on a stream or lake.

⊚ Make paper airplanes and fly them.

⊚ See how many ways you can have fun with a cardboard box.

⊚ Buy the latest issue of MAD Magazine or a comic book and read all of it in one shot.

⊚ Watch cartoons on a Saturday morning.

⊚ Build a model ship, plane, or car.

⊚ Play with a rubber duck in the bath.

⊚ Go fly a kite on a windy day.

⊚ Read a children's book.

⊚ Buy a coloring book and color away to your heart's content. Use the worst colors possible.

Pay close attention to the law of detrimental returns as it relates to work and studying. More than eight or ten hours of work a day can harm your health. Studies have shown that people who work normal work hours are the most productive and that the best marks are earned by students who study moderate amounts.

Make a point of reading books and magazines that are totally unrelated to your work. Read for the pleasure of reading and not for the purpose of learning something to aid you in your job.

To add more fun to your life and other people's lives, learn and tell as many good jokes as you can with which you can liven up a conversation.

The menu at the Ritz Diner in Edmonton, Canada, advises, "If you're not served in 5 minutes, you'll be served in 8 or 9 . . . maybe 12 minutes. RELAX!"

Don't forget to try doing some of the kid things that you never did.

Some things need doing better than you or anyone has ever done them before. Some just need doing to get by. Some are not necessary; they don't need doing at all. Learn to distinguish between the three.

When's the last time you went dancing? Head out to a dance hall, nightclub, or church function this weekend. Dancing is a great way to relieve stress.

Be prepared to take spontaneous two- or three-day minivacations at a moment's notice. Have your bags packed so there is no delay.

Climb at least one mountain in your lifetime. Your experience of life and time will take on new dimensions.

Ride your bicycle to the store or office. Enjoy the trees and the birds and the green grass and the pretty flowers and the fresh air and . . . .

It's a waste of your precious time observing what your neighbors are doing. Do something interesting and satisfying so your neighbors end up wasting their time observing what *you* are doing.

An unknown wise person said, "Yesterday is history, tomorrow is a mystery, and today is a gift; that's why it's called the present." In other words, at this moment you can't celebrate yesterday, neither can you celebrate tomorrow, so why not celebrate today?

**For a new source of joy in your life,
laugh at nothing in particular.**

Just once in your life, take a thousand dollars or five thousand dollars and let the good times roll. Take a trip to some city such as San Francisco just for the sake of having a good time. Tell them I sent you.

Spend a day with an active senior citizen who still has an incredible zest for life. Note the qualities of this person, most likely to include adaptive, creative, spontaneous, friendly, inquisitive, playful, independent, and the ability to act crazy. Are you developing and maintaining these qualities, too, so that you can really enjoy life?

Cut yourself a little slack in your day. Every so often stare into space without a clear purpose.

Check out your "To Do" list. How many leisure pursuits does it include? If you are living a balanced lifestyle, it should include at least a few.

Start each day in a special way. Get up early and go for a walk before you go to work. Then play your favorite tune on the piano or stereo.

End each day in a special way. Have a glass of wine or two with some cheese while you read a good book before going to bed.

Have at least one leisure activity in which you can get totally immersed. Make sure there is no deadline for completing this activity.

Ask your travel agent to notify you of any special travel deals so you can take advantage of cheap rates to leave town and relax.

For a good break away from work, visit an exotic place such as Nepal. Hiking through the Himalayas for a week or two will rejuvenate your soul.

In addition to sunsets, stop and watch more sunrises. Get up earlier if you have to.

The darkest hour is the one just before the sun rises. When you are feeling down, keep these words of Will Rogers in mind: "Things will get better—despite our efforts to improve them."

One out of every two American adults suffers from sleep deprivation, yet a study of navy personnel indicates that people who are well rested make considerably more money. Of course, with more earning power, you will have more time for leisure because you require less time for making a living.

Be cultured and support your local performers at the same time. When is the last time you went to the symphony, opera, or ballet?

Be more spontaneous. Have thirty minutes or so of unstructured time every day to do something unplanned and different. Notice how your life is enriched.

Evaluate your friendships to ensure that you aren't putting in a lot more than you're getting out of them. Don't hesitate to end old friendships that are causing more stress and discomfort than they are worth. Simply drift out of those that are no longer working for you.

Researchers confirm strenuous exercise calms the mind. Try going for a long walk or walking up and down a flight of stairs several times. Strenuous exercise will not only reduce your stress but may also prevent you from getting stressed out in the first place.

Keep in mind the words of Yogi Berra: "You can observe a lot just by watching." Stop functioning on automatic pilot. Make a concerted effort to pay more attention. If you really look, you will see 101 interesting and exciting things happening in the world around you.

Take the time to really listen actively to others. An unknown wise person said it best, "You don't learn anything when you are talking."

**Make every one of your birthdays an all-day celebration.**

To enhance the quality of your life, get out of your car as much as possible. It's an isolation device that shields you from nature and people.

Get yourself a T-shirt with your favorite cartoon figure. Wear it often.

Stop, listen, enjoy, and make a contribution to the local buskers. Many of these street musicians are incredibly talented and deserve your acknowledgment.

If you are so bored that you would get excited about an invitation to the opening of an envelope, ask yourself what is responsible for your boredom. Here's a hint: Dylan Thomas said, "Somebody is boring me; I think it is me."

It takes many years to become an overnight success. Develop patience for everything you do. Shoot for conquering the world by the year 2010 instead of 2001.

Misery doesn't only love company, it demands it. If you find yourself in the company of someone who regularly drains your energy, it's not wise to stick around. Don't walk away from negative people—RUN!

Learn how to enjoy your own company so that any time spent alone is satisfying and productive. Practice spending a whole day by yourself at least twice a year to help you learn what makes you tick.

Take the time (a day or two) to write down what you're really looking for in life. Identify the things that are the most important to you. Make them the purpose and focus of your existence.

F eel more alive by getting out of the house more often and sampling good opportunities life has to offer. When was the last time you went to the art gallery, museum, or planetarium? If it has been a long time, go today.

T ruly enjoy and experience a sunset by painting a picture of it. Don't judge the skill of your efforts. Revel in the experience.

**Wisdom is a journey and not a destination.**

C hoose to spend time with optimistic instead of pessimistic individuals. You will discover you are more enthusiastic about life.

Do something outrageous—every week—anything totally out of character for you.

Don't put off the joy of living. In other words, don't postpone having fun. Make it part of your regular routine.

*Active* leisure is pursuing a challenging task that gives you great pleasure and satisfaction in its completion. So instead of heading down to the bingo or gambling hall, learn a new language and see the difference.

Jeff Gould of the Gould Morning Show on WSN-AM radio in Sioux Falls, South Dakota has declared July 20 as National Nap Day. On this day take the time to have a long, relaxing nap.

If you have a career that is going nowhere, and deep down you have known it for quite some time, you must start exploring new ways to make a living immediately. Don't let unfavorable odds keep you from pursuing what you know intuitively you were meant to do.

For a different and relaxing experience, go to the park and find a comfortable place to sit or lie down. Close your eyes and concentrate on the sounds of your surroundings. Concentrate on the smells, as well.

Life is short, so don't spend too much time stuffing mushrooms. Some things are important and some aren't. It's essential that you know how to tell the difference. Failure to do so can cause all sorts of disillusionment and waste in your life.

Be unpredictable. Do something different. It's okay to be unpredictable so that others are surprised by your actions.

Invest in your family first and your career second. Stop taking your spouse for granted when working overtime at the office. Relationships and families are high maintenance. Many relationships have ended because of a workaholic spouse forgetting to devote time to the relationship and the kids.

Keep track of where you expend your time, money, energy, and creativity. If you are expending too much of one or more resources inefficiently, it's time to make a change.

Create more slack in your days. You don't have to plan the time in every day right down to the minute. If your day-timer is jammed full, reduce the number of activities you are trying to cram into each day.

Rain doesn't have to put a damper on your leisure activities. Take a rainy afternoon to celebrate your good fortune in life by reviewing all the photographs you have accumulated.

Get immersed in a real conversation with your neighbor that has a natural starting time and a natural finishing time not dictated by the clock.

Cherish old memories; however, don't forget to create new ones today that you will be able to savor tomorrow.

Pay little attention to what others are doing in life. Just because the majority is doing something, doesn't make it wise. In fact, the masses are frequently misguided in their pursuit of happiness and satisfaction.

A *Globe and Mail* article cited the example set by Richard Israels of Vancouver, a man who died of colon cancer in 1997 at the age of fifty-one. Even in the last few months of his life, this man did not lament over his unfortunate affliction. Owing to his exuberance, he had found his relatively short life exciting and satisfying. He reflected just before his death, "No matter what, I had a good run." Prepare yourself everyday for the time you will have to go so that you will be able to say that you had a good run at life.

Quit whining. It is a waste of energy. Be more constructive with your time. Focus on what's right with the world, instead of what's wrong with it.

Take a bicycle trip of a hundred miles or more where you will be exposed to the elements—to all the sights, sounds, and smells along the way. You will experience myriad things you can never experience traveling the same route in a car.

At least once a day, display those traits you had when you were a child. Children are imaginative, playful, curious, and spontaneous.

Don't take your worries and problems to bed with you. To fight insomnia keep an inspirational book or two handy by your bedside.

Use your humor and zest for living to transform a gloomy morning into a beautiful one. You can change the quality of your life by changing the context in which you view your circumstances. Make an effort to put a positive slant on even the gloomiest events.

**Be a child again. Enjoy the world for all it is worth.**

Add novelty to your life as much as possible. Researchers at the University of Southern California found that individuals who regularly do new things, such as going to places they have never been or playing a new game, were happier and had a greater sense of well-being than people who keep doing the same old things.

Don't ever forget this important point if you want a more balanced lifestyle: You don't have to work hard to make a decent living, but you may have to work smarter.

Tell the truth about whether you are a workaholic by seeing whether any of these symptoms apply to you:

- You spend more than forty-five hours a week at work and get paid for only forty.

- You seldom or never take all your vacation entitlement.

- You use work to avoid social commitments.

- Work is a substitute for hobbies and other leisure interests.

- Work life interferes with family life.

- You postpone fun things.

- You are more than willing to fill any free time by undertaking other people's projects.

Play street hockey or try skateboarding with a group of ten-year-olds and experience life from their perspective.

Share a job if you are working too hard and your personal life is suffering. Job sharing has helped tens of thousands of people to bring their lives back to a better balance.

**Find a tree to lie under and read a novel for an hour or two.**

Make a list of your dreams and analyze them. Are you spending the appropriate time on achieving your dreams? The ache of unfulfilled dreams can be the worst pain you ever experience. Yet dreams often do come true for those who focus and work on them.

Retire early so you have more time for living. You don't need a million dollars to retire. Many people have retired at thirty or forty with only $250,000 or less to their name.

Health professionals state that deep breathing is important for optimum health. Stop and take five deep breaths of fresh air when you go outside in the morning.

Cloud formations are fascinating. Have you laid on your back and watched clouds since you were a kid? Why not? Just do it.

Share and experience the everyday lives of people around the world by staying with a host family. Servas, an international network in New York for hosts and travelers, can arrange this for you.

Drink expensive wine or good champagne at least once a month—whether or not you have something to celebrate.

If you dislike going to parties, don't go just because you feel obligated. Spend your time doing what you like doing.

Take a year off and work yourself around the world. Here are two books that tell you how: *Work Yourself Around the World* and *Teaching English Abroad* (Peterson's Publishing).

Don't send Christmas or Hanukkah cards just because everyone else does. Send special cards in February when you have more time and they will be better appreciated.

Try to escape from the kids for at least a whole day once a month. One way is to send the kids to summer camp while you and your spouse head off on a separate vacation.

Hang out at the largest magazine stand in your area. Browse through magazines on as many different topics as you can—anything from cooking to sewing to golf to cycling to cruising to windsurfing. This may trigger some new activity you would like to try.

Constantly question advertisers who tell you that their products will make your life better. How much better can it get due to more possessions if you can't find the time to enjoy what you already have? Be governed by your own inner needs instead of outside influences.

Refrain from trying to be a know-it-all. You don't have to be an expert on every subject imaginable. Besides, know-it-alls are a pain to most people.

Work at maintaining a healthy weight. Be in control over food instead of allowing food to control you. You will be in better shape to work more efficiently and enjoy life more.

One of the signs of inner peace is the ability to be nonjudgmental of oneself and others. Spend one whole day focusing on being nonjudgmental of people.

It's the small things you do that make life worth living. Take the time to smile and say hello to people you don't know to show them how much you appreciate life.

If friendship is lacking in your life, follow the advice of Ralph Waldo Emerson: "The only way to have a friend is to be one."

If you are married, be more romantic with your spouse more often. Being romantic is an attitude that comes from the soul and spirit—not a lot of money. Try reading Gregory J. P. Godeck's *1001 Ways to Be Romantic* (Casablanca Press).

Here's some telling words from Merry Browne on how well you are doing with your life: "If you want an accounting of your worth, count your friends."

Hasty decisions can get you into trouble. Often important decisions should be put off as long as possible. The extra time you take may save you money or help you come up with a much more effective solution.

Stop trying to read everything. If you are suffering from information overload, cancel some of your magazine subscriptions.

Pamper yourself regularly. Small rewards, such as dining out, are much more satisfying and effective than large rewards, such as an expensive outfit or a new car.

Find the time to have a backyard barbecue for your neighbors at least once a year, especially if they are great neighbors. If they are lousy neighbors, channel your energy elsewhere.

Remember there is no perfect solution to any problem. Stop trying to find it.

It's wise to avoid being overly goal oriented and judging yourself totally on work-related or materialistic accomplishments. At the end of the day, determine how well your day went also by how much you relaxed, laughed, and played.

Remind yourself that life will be a series of adventures and wonderful discoveries if you are creative with your leisure time. To get in touch with your creativity, read *The Artist's Way* by Julia Cameron.

To feel happy, relaxed, and at peace with the world, you must be able to sit back and let life take its natural course. Learn to go with the flow more. Let things happen instead of always trying to make things happen.

Take the time to immerse yourself totally in the forgotten art of handwriting letters to friends and relatives. Be creative. Be outrageous. Be funny. You will get a great deal of satisfaction from displaying your creativity.

A sk your friends to question some of your activities that seem unnecessary or more complicated than they should be. Your friends may see some opportunity where you may see none.

O n December 31 of every year, congratulate yourself for making it through the year. Review your successes and pat yourself on the back.

W rite a book on one of your favorite subjects. To maintain momentum and accomplishment, write at least fifteen minutes a day. Once you have finished, self-publish only ten or twenty copies for starters.

Eliminate all distractions when you are doing something important such as writing a book or making love. Shut off the television, disconnect the phone, and ignore—even disconnect—the doorbell.

Create your own little black book of humorous, witty, and inspirational quotes. When you are feeling down or dejected, read these quotations to give yourself a lift.

You can't win all the time no matter how good you are. Therefore, refrain from always trying to be better than others at work and play. Egotism is trying to prove you are worthwhile because deep down you feel you are not.

In this hurried world it's much too easy to allow solid friendships to languish. Don't take your friends for granted. Make the time to telephone and visit them, or you may end up losing them.

Lighten up! Oscar Wilde said, "Life is much too important to be taken seriously." At times forget about the serious matters altogether. Talking about the lighter side of life will ease the stress that comes from the serious side.

**Never be too busy to help a good friend who is in need.**

July 22 is Summer Leisure Day. Make sure that at least half your day is spent on leisure.

Ensure that you get up early enough to eat a leisurely break-fast before you go to work. Eating in the car on the way to work is both unhealthy and dangerous.

If you feel that life is getting the best of you, take a slower than normal pace for a week and see what happens to your stress level.

Don't allow inevitable days when career, financial, or personal matters are not as bright as you would like to detract from all the good things happening in your life.

Refrain from taking it with you to restaurants, golf courses, parks, and while indulging in other leisure activities. The "it" is your cell phone. Your enjoyment of life will be greatly enhanced if you use your cell phone only when it's absolutely necessary to receive a certain phone call.

If you can afford it, hire a housecleaning service so that you have more time for the important things in life. You will also be helping out the employees of the service by giving them some work and income.

Your mother was right: take your time to make sure that you chew your food properly. Properly digested food is necessary for good health. The importance of eating slowly and deliberately to totally absorb the energy from the food is also emphasized in *The Celestine Prophecy.*

Because there are truly no stupid questions, make every day Ask a Stupid Question Day. This will ensure that you keep learning about the world around you. Aristotle said, "When you ask a dumb question, you get a smart answer."

Depending on how you handle and reduce stress in your life, you can end up being a bright light, a flickering one, or a complete burnout. The Health Resources Network has declared April as Stress Awareness Month, but try to always be aware of how stress can interfere with your health. Contact your doctor for more information.

Never neglect a sick friend or relative. Bring them flowers, a card, and a special gift. Share your time and laughter and try to cheer them up.

Take the time to discover what you are passionate about. Make a list of your favorite cities, resorts, sports, games, songs, wine, authors, movies, restaurants, and food. Incorporate these things into your leisure activities.

If you have a fireplace in your house, use it. This is a time to be romantic or to relax by gazing into the fire with nothing on your mind.

If someone has influenced you to get upset, tell yourself, "So what!" One thing that will hold you back in life is wasting energy on things better forgotten. If you are contemplating some drastic move, at least wait a few days. You may decide that it's not worth the trouble.

Vary what you do on weekends. Don't get into a routine. Here's a suggestion: Instead of eating the normal breakfast at home, head out on a side road you have never traveled and eat at the first interesting restaurant you encounter.

Ensure that the majority of your friends are not associated with your workplace. Nonwork friends provide a much broader exchange of life and the world.

For relief of stress, try scream therapy. When alone at home or in your car on the freeway scream to your heart's content. You will notice the difference immediately.

Ovid said, "Happy is the man who can count his sufferings." Instead of thinking about your problems, once in a while think of all the severe problems you have been spared and how much tougher your life could be.

Arguing over something trivial wastes time and energy that could be utilized doing some real living. Sing to your spouse instead of nagging or arguing with him or her. You'll both feel better.

Never neglect your parents due to your busy lifestyle. Call your mother and father at least once a week no matter where you are or how busy you are.

If you are in your car complaining about the heavy traffic, remember you are to blame for it as much as any other vehicle on the road at that time. Stop driving and you will see your heavy traffic problem disappear quickly.

# Money and Happiness

Be clear about the purpose of money. Money is like health. It is necessary for survival, but it is not what you live for.

Don't admire people for their wealth. Admire people for the great things they have been able to accomplish, such as attaining peace and happiness, despite their lack of wealth.

When you are considering buying something, ask yourself how many hours you will have to work to pay for it. Is it worth it?

Watch less TV and you will spend less money. Juliet Schor, in her book *The Overspent American* (Basic Books), concludes that the more TV a person watches, the more likely he or she is to spend and live beyond his or her means.

**Buy quality instead of luxury or style.**

Remember that many of the best things in life are free or cost very little. A University of Chicago study confirmed that people get the most pleasure and satisfaction from inexpensive leisure activities.

Rethink the meaning of security. *Security* comes from the Latin word *securus,* meaning "without care." To be truly secure in this world, you must learn to be without care whether you have a lot of money or are on a limited budget. Others with more money than you may not be as secure.

Live your life as a spiritual being not principally as a con- sumer.

Just because something is fashionable does not mean it is worthy of your attention and money. Don't be a slave to the dictates of fashion critics by wearing trendy clothes just to fit in. Instead of adopting someone else's image, show your true personality and wear something inexpensive, but truly differ- ent and creative. Dress for others' approval only if they are prepared to pay for it.

Eliminate unrealistic expectations of what a great amount of money can do for you. If money makes people happy, then why do the British Royal Family have so many problems? Think of all the people you know who are making a lot of money but are in constant crises and aren't enjoying life.

It is not as important to increase your possessions as it is to scale down your wants. Eliminating your desire for something is as good as possessing it, and often less trouble. The key is to live below your means. Instead of striving to keep up with the Joneses, find greater contentment in living more simply.

Making hasty decisions when making major purchases can be financially disastrous. Take at least a day or two to think it over.

Make sure your expectations for "the good life" are in line with reality. You may have to rein in your desires by staying away from the malls and not reading the magazines espousing the more expensive displays of "the good life."

If you don't want to work so hard, abide by one of the following secrets for handling money: The first powerful way to handle money is to spend less than you earn. If this doesn't work for you, then the second one is for you: Earn more than you spend.

Look at the broader long-term picture—try to succeed at the things that really count for emotional fulfillment. Being obsessed with getting rich and beating everyone at the game of acquiring material wealth will not leave you fulfilled.

Waste no time or energy envying others or coveting their possessions. Envy is like acid; it eats away the container that it's in. There will always be friends, relatives, neighbors, or celebrities, who own bigger houses, drive flashier cars, or wear more expensive clothes.

Instead of ordinary gifts that cost money, give your family the gift of time. This gift will go a lot further than material gifts in showing your love.

Be aware of the dangers of greed. Whether it's greed for promotions, material possessions, money, or popularity, it will come back to haunt you. One of the ways greed gets back at you is by robbing you of precious time.

Separate your actual needs from your wants. Most of what we preconceive as needs are really wants and not real needs. Reduce spending on your wants, and you won't have to work so hard.

If you have a substantial sum of money, learn to enjoy it instead of leaving it for someone else to enjoy. Keep in mind the words of the unknown wise person who said, "It is better to live rich than to die rich."

In fact, try to spend *all* your money before you die. According to Stephen Pollan, author of *Die Broke,* the ideal is to have your last check written to the undertaker bounce. Then in your will you can write: "I, being of sound mind, spent all my money while I was still alive."

Before you buy something, ask yourself how much you will actually use it. Consider whether you can borrow it from a friend or relative.

Keep your overhead low. Cut down expenses and have "a high joy-to-stuff ratio" by reading *Your Money or Your Life* by Joe Dominguez and Vicki Robin. This powerful book has helped tens of thousands of people get their financial lives in order so they have to work less.

Pay heed to this important advice from Kay Lyons: "Yesterday is a canceled check, tomorrow is a promissory note; today is the only cash you have—so spend it wisely."

Your creativity and ability to generate new ideas to deal with life's problems has to be worth over $1 million. The day you start fully tapping your creative abilities is the day you start yourself on the road to being able to take it easy while others toil long hours for a living.

If you are pressed for time to relax, don't be penny wise and dollar foolish. Spending two or three hours driving across town to save a few dollars is crazy. Your time and sanity are worth much more than that.

Put money in its place. Money can buy you cars, houses, trinkets, fleeting sex, shallow companionship, cheap attention, and unfulfilled status. However, it can't buy you peace, love, or happiness.

Consider that spending money wisely on a limited income and saving more can be more productive and powerful than earning more money. Don't forget your own ingenuity in saving and spending your money wisely. Make a list of the many things you can do to handle money so you don't have to work as hard to acquire it.

Accept that you will never have enough money to solve all your problems. If you can't accept this, then you aren't clear about money. People with a great amount of money have just as many problems as the rest of us—sometimes more. Just read the daily newspapers and you pay attention to all the trouble rich people are in.

Pay attention to what you do with your money on a daily basis. Keep a written record of what you spend money on, and how much, every day for a week.

Get smart financially. Read as many books on saving money, taxes, financial planning, and investments as you can get your hands on so that you are knowledgeable about how to handle money.

Never lend a large amount of money to a friend or relative (50 percent of loans to family members and 75 percent of loans to friends aren't paid back). If the friend has a hard time paying you back, you will lose both your money and your friendship. Banks exist to provide financial support; friendships exist for nonfinancial support.

E nrich and simplify your life by subscribing to *Simple Living—The Journal of Voluntary Simplicity* (Seattle, Washington).

**Earn your dollars before you spend them.**

G et your hands on *The Tightwad Gazette,* volumes 1, 2, and 3 (Villard Books) by Amy Dacyczyn. These three books are a compilation of hundreds of ways to save money that appeared in previous issues of her newsletter of the same name.

N ever compromise your honesty to make money, even if it appears that you are the only one playing by the rules. If you make $10 dishonestly, it will cost you $100 later on—not necessarily in pure financial terms but in the loss of self-respect and the respect of others, not to mention possible time in jail.

If you enjoy browsing and exploring in your leisure time, then use some of your time away from work to visit second-hand stores, auctions, flea markets, and garage sales. You'll save money by finding gifts and practical items that could cost you a lot more elsewhere.

Stay away from gambling of any kind. Wilson Mizner defined gambling as "The sure way of getting nothing for something."

Consider getting rid of your car to save an amazing amount of money. In Vancouver, for example, a new car costs an average of $595 a month to run. (Remember you may have to gross $1,000 a month to net $595.) To help your transition to a car-free life, subscribe to the *Auto-Free Times*.

Learn to give some of your money away. This will enhance your prosperity consciousness and allow you to enjoy your life more.

Don't be a miser or hoarder. Spending a certain portion of your money—some even frivolously—is important for maintaining a healthy attitude about money and life. Enjoying your money and life will help you accumulate more money.

Give consideration to these powerful statements about money by Michael Phillips in his book *The Seven Laws of Money:*

- Money creates and maintains its own rules.

- Money will appear when you are doing the right thing in your life.

- Money is a dream—in fact, it can be a fantasy as deceptive as the Pied Piper.

- Money often is a nightmare.

- You can never truly give money away as a gift.

- You can never truly receive money as a gift.

- There are many fascinating worlds without money.

Go one step further with your credit cards. Don't ever use them for credit. Use them for convenience and to acquire air miles. Pay the bills immediately.

Don't hang around with the Joneses and you won't have to keep up with them. Since we tend to adopt the values and beliefs of the people around us, hang around people who are more in tune with voluntary simplicity, have a good work/life balance, and are making the world a better place to live.

Extend yourself financially to purchase a house but never do so for a car.

Before you purchase some more clothes, gadgets, or trinkets that you probably don't need, consider that the average American and Canadian consumes five times more than a Mexican, ten times more than a Chinese person, and thirty times more than a person in India.

Use these six basic ways to save money:

- ⚙ Buy it for less.

- ⚙ Use it less.

- ⚙ Maintain it and take good care of it so it lasts longer.

- ⚙ Try to fix the old before buying a new replacement.

- ⚙ Buy it in partnership with someone else.

- ⚙ Don't buy it at all.

Note that being frugal is not being cheap or stingy. The word *frugal* comes from Latin words associated with virtue and value and the verb *to enjoy*.

If you save enough money to live without work for a year, you won't have to feel trapped in a job. Put aside some money from every paycheck into a "Take This Job and Shove It" fund.

Establish a separate bank account for frivolous spending. Put away 2 percent to 5 percent of your income for items that you don't need but would truly like to have. When you have enough money, buy one of these items. Make sure you spend all the money in this account frivolously.

Don't put yourself under undue stress by believing what some money financial planners say you need to retire. These figures are normally based on a consumer lifestyle that is not necessary for fulfillment and happiness. The less you live on while you are working, the less you will need for retirement.

When spending money on any item, spend only as much as you have to and as little as you can get away with.

Don't buy something just to be cool. *Cool* and *intelligent* are not synonymous. The urge to be cool has driven many people into personal bankruptcy.

Learn to say no to your children. Children make a habit out of asking for more and more money or things. If they use the rationale that all the other kids have it, acknowledge their want but be firm that they don't *need* it.

Explain to your children that even the poor in the United States and Canada live considerably better than people in other nations and a lot better than people did fifty or a hundred years ago. The important point to make is that contentment depends on how much we appreciate what we have, instead of how much we have.

Keep in mind that the more things you buy, the less time you will have to enjoy the things you already have.

Don't economize in an attempt to leave money for your adult children after you die. Adult children should be self-sufficient as soon as they leave home and not require economic out-patient care.

**Learn to think of opportunity instead of security.**

The day after Thanksgiving Day has been declared Buy Nothing Day by the voluntary simplicity movement. Try to go through the whole day without making any purchases, and invest whatever money you would normally have spent on this day in your retirement fund.

Create your own list of ways you can enjoy free things and activities. Here's some to get you started:

- Go to wine tastings at wine stores.

- Have a snack at grocery stores that feature free samples.

- Pick flowers on the side of a road to give to your lover.

- Volunteer at theater groups, jazz clubs, and other entertainment venues to see free performances.

- Pets are expensive, don't buy one. Instead, borrow your neighbor's dog and take it for a walk.

- Have a party at your house. Ask everyone to bring food and drinks. Don't contribute anything yourself except for the house.

- Watch your local newspapers for open houses of jazz clubs and theatre groups. Many open houses offer free admission, and the performances are first-class.

- Subscribe to *The Caretaker Gazette* and find out how you can sign up as a property caretaker and live rent-free in great places: farms, ranches, camps, and nature preserves. Write to 1845 NW Deane St., Pullman, WA, 99163-3509.

Pay heed to the words of Mahatma Gandhi: "The world has enough for everyone's need, but not enough for everyone's greed."

Try integrating your material needs with your spiritual needs. Purchase things that speak of your essence and not of the wishes of your friends or advertisers.

**Don't buy something just because it is on sale.**

Slow down in your drive to have a big investment portfolio. Patience should overrule greed. Buy stocks in good companies and hold onto them for a long time.

Only invest in risky ventures the amount of money you are prepared to part with for good.

Look at a limited income as a blessing in disguise. This gives you a chance to be creative and live within your means. Many well-off married couples say they were much happier when they had less and had to be creative to get by financially.

Pay attention to what the Buddhists advise: "Want what you have and you will always get what you want."

If you don't have as much money as others you know, stop lamenting your fate. Envy and jealousy will only serve to keep you resentful and choke off the energy required to make a positive change in your life.

Remember the difference between spending 10 percent more than you earn and spending 10 percent less than you earn translates, respectively, into financial chaos and eventual personal bankruptcy versus financial satisfaction and personal freedom.

Ask yourself, "What is the point of giving my kids the good life of excess materialism if they aren't getting what's really important for their well-being?" Your children require more than anything else your affection, love, psychological security, and guidance.

Be prepared to enjoy your money, especially if you are in the higher income bracket. If you have never been to a restaurant that doesn't have trays, now is the time to get over your poverty consciousness and start living.

# The Workplace

Don't let your ego and beliefs about the value of working hard stand in the way of your experience of life. Be willing to resist traditional ways of thinking. By being more open-minded, we find that our personalities and way of life don't have to be cast in stone.

If you must call the office while on vacation, limit your telephone calls to just one a day. Have the staff at the office be prepared in advance of your one call to discuss the things that must be discussed.

Keep in mind that working eight or more hours a day is not natural for human beings. The forty-hour work week came with the Industrial Revolution. In primitive societies (which I consider more advanced), people worked an average of three or four hours a day.

If you are working long hours to become rich and famous, ask yourself, "Do I want to be the richest, most famous person in the graveyard?"

Challenge your need to spend time networking at work-related associations or functions after work hours. A cover story in *Fortune* magazine about highly successful female executives found that they did not spend time networking because they did not find it important for success.

Ensure that your job is serving you instead of you serving your job. Your work should energize you and give meaning to your life. If it isn't, consider making a change. Find something that will stretch your talents more.

**Say something positive the moment you enter your workplace.**

If you ever find yourself unemployed, look at this time as an opportunity. Being unemployed is the true test of who you really are. Take your time getting back in the workforce. Don't just settle for a job; wait for the right opportunity.

On a daily basis, keep challenging your belief that hard work is a virtue. Many people have kept their noses to the grindstone for thirty or forty years and wound up with nothing more than a flat nose.

To be well read on a tight schedule, incorporate reading into other activities where possible. Read while using a stationary exercise bicycle or while waiting for the bus.

If you must commute a long distance, use this time wisely. Don't listen to any radio shows that cause you to feel stress or to think in a negative way. Instead, listen to relaxing music, good novels on tapes, or self-help tapes.

Commuting long distances—more than thirty minutes away—is an incredible waste of natural resources and human energy. By reducing your commuting time, not only will your car have less wear and tear, your body will also.

Announce to the world that you don't accept business calls at home.

Hewlett Packard recently started a campaign to persuade its hundred thousand workers to have a better balance between work and play. Susan Moriconi, head of the company's Work/Life program, states that long hours and unnecessary business trips reduce creativity and wear down employees emotionally and physically.

THE DARK SIDE OF PUNCTUALITY

When you get into the office, handle your toughest task first. This will reduce your stress and anxiety since you won't have to think about it later in the day.

Delegate some tasks even if it means they don't get done as thoroughly or finished as quickly. You will be able to go home earlier to pursue leisure activities and spend time with your family. You will also have more time on the job for creativity and to generate new opportunities.

Operate out of excellence—not perfection. Do the best you can within the allotted time and then move on.

Enhance your job by looking at what you can do differently. What can you change that will make it easier for you to complete your tasks within regular work hours?

Once or twice a year, on the spur-of-the-moment opt out by taking a half day off to go golfing or sailing.

Humorless workers are a real drag. Make sure that you exercise your sense of humor at work in a way that cheers others and yourself at the same time.

No matter how frustrated you get, keep a tight rein on your temper. When you allow someone to make you angry, you have let them control you.

Minimize work activities that you dislike. Working too much at things you don't like will interfere with your performance, health, and sense of well-being.

If you aren't getting anything out of that Leadership 2000 Seminar, leave early to pursue something leisurely. Don't feel obligated to stay until the end of a seminar or management training program to which your company has sent you.

Put funny and entertaining cartoons relating to the workplace on memos, fax messages, bulletin boards, office walls, and doors.

According to *Celebrate Today,* April 3 is Don't Go to Work Unless It's Fun Day. If you are one of the two-thirds of Americans who don't enjoy your job, this is the day to stay home and reflect on what you would really like to do for a living.

A 1997 study conducted by the Institute for the Future, the Gallup Organization, and San Jose State University in California found employees of Fortune 1000 companies used a number of guerrilla tactics to handle message overload at the office. Here's one: Don't empty your voice mailbox and you won't get more messages.

From the same study, here's another guerilla tactic to handle message overload: Let your cell phone batteries run low so you can't receive more calls.

See if you can implement this tactic in your organization for being more efficient and getting more work done: an hour or two of quiet time every day during which employees are allowed to work and not be interrupted by telephone calls, e-mail, visits by coworkers, and sales calls by outsiders.

When Bob Waterman, coauthor of *In Search of Excellence,* worked at Bank of America, he would occasionally give his workers the afternoon off to go enjoy the sunshine. If you are a manager or business owner, do the same. If you are an employee, try to convince your boss to do the same.

Learn to daydream at work without being caught. Daydreaming can be relaxing and productive. Your creativity will be enhanced.

Consider making your office more spiritual. Read *Altars Made Easy: A Complete Guide to Creating Your Own Sacred Place* by Peg Streep, who says, "Carving out a sacred place at the office is an effort to integrate all parts of ourselves and help us to connect with who we really are."

**Try to work in the area that gives you the most natural light.**

Have something therapeutic in sight at all times. This can be your favorite plant or a mini water fountain.

Keep in mind that there is no prize for having your car be the first one to enter the company parking lot and be the last one to leave.

Certain scents make us more relaxed and productive. Read up on aromatherapy, and then place your favorite aromas in your office and breathe them in when you are feeling stressed. The aromas along with your pausing to take deep breaths will rejuvenate your spirit.

Take a sabbatical from work every five years or so. Start a sabbatical bank account now, and in a few years you can have a break of six months or more away from work.

Put work in its place. Sure, you have to make a living. Why make it an obsession? Work should be a part of daily living but not more important than play.

Don't resist change—adapt to it. You will be happier and more relaxed. Consider that most of the time change leads to something better in the long run.

If feeling good is the one thing you need in your life more than anything else, tonight go somewhere where the people are pleasant and the music is great. The work at the office can wait.

Spend as much time as you can with leisurely people. Once a month invite someone to lunch who enjoys life more than you do.

If you are having a bad day at the workplace, get some exercise on the job by walking around or climbing a few flights of stairs. Exercise will calm your mind and give you a greater sense of well being.

As with personal matters, practice making quicker decisions on trivial or insignificant issues at work. Here again, flip a coin if it's easier. The time you save can be spent on happier pursuits.

To have a better balance between work and play, borrow a tactic from Hewlett Packard. The company asks its employees to ask themselves what value a task will bring and what will happen if employees don't do it. To reduce your workload, challenge whether you really have to generate that extra report or arrange another meeting.

A workplace poster states, "For stress relief, just bang your head on the wall three times." DON'T DO THIS! Find other creative ways to relieve stress, such as playing street hockey in the parking lot at noon.

**Play your favorite background music to help alleviate stress.**

Consider the idea of a nap room again. A recent article in the *Washington Post* reported that some companies have nap rooms to enhance their employees' health and creativity. Not only does the company allow employees to take naps, it encourages it.

Don't wait for others to make your workplace pleasant and fun. Instigate the fun for others.

Take the time to celebrate your own and your coworkers' birthdays and anniversaries by decorating the workplace and going out for lunch.

May 31, the birthday of Johnny Paycheck, is "Take This Job and Shove It Day." Use this day to quit your job if you hate it.

Pace yourself effectively when undertaking new projects. Throwing yourself at the task at hand may seem the right thing to do initially but it will be the wrong thing in the long run. You will end up wasting time and energy.

Get outside as much as you can! Take advantage of any opportunity you have to leave the office or the building in which you work. The sunlight and outside air are better for you than the light and air in buildings.

Whatever you do at home, don't regularly stay up into the wee hours of the night. Staying up too late can ruin your energy level and cognitive skills for the next day.

If you follow a monotonous and boring routine everyday when you leave work—drive home, change clothes, prepare dinner, wash dishes, watch TV, and go to bed—then divert drastically from your routine at least once a week.

Wear the most comfortable clothes in the office that you can get away with. There's no point making yourself uncomfortable with a tie or tight shoes because you or someone else thinks you look better in these clothes.

If you can get away with it, take off your shoes and give your feet a good rest. Put your feet up on the desk, while you're at it!

Try to integrate your personal beliefs with your line of work. Your work should reflect your higher self or essence. The biggest contributing factor to job burnout is a mismatch between personal and corporate values.

If you think you have a lousy job, stop feeling sorry for yourself. Find something better as soon as you can. Subscribe to *Changing Course Magazine* (www.changingcourse.com) for creative alternatives to the nine-to-five work world, practical how-to advice, and inspiration to help you live a simpler, more balanced life working at what you love.

Since the urge to have an afternoon nap is a natural, biologically driven tendency, get your company to have a nap room. Workplace researchers confirm naps enhance safety, creativity, production, morale, and overall performance.

When you can't take a nap at work, try to catch forty winks here and there. As an alternative, learn to meditate at work. Even five minutes a day at work will give you increased energy.

Too much mental work will sever your mind from your body. A half hour of aerobic exercise will do the trick. Use dancing, yoga, or jogging to get your mind in touch with your body.

Bring some of your favorite toys to work. Playing with them on stressful days will make you more relaxed and productive.

Greg Goddeck, author of *1001 Ways to Be More Romantic,* advises that you should take the time from your work to phone your partner at least once a day and let him or her know you aren't only thinking about work all day.

According to a 1997 survey, more than 55 percent of U.S. workers take fifteen minutes or less for lunch. This is both unhealthy and counterproductive. Ensure that you are taking sufficient time to eat and digest your food. Go for a walk after lunch, too.

The same survey indicated that 63 percent of U.S. workers skip lunch at least once a week. If you are one of these people, quit this unhealthy habit, especially if you aren't getting paid extra for working during your lunch hour.

Let go of the habit of regularly using all of your lunch break to run personal errands. This will leave you just as exhausted as working throughout lunch without eating.

Arrange a weekly event with your coworkers during lunch hours to help relieve stress and put more fun into your workday. For example, show home videos or slides from exotic vacations.

Use part of your lunch hour for spiritual renewal. Regularly retreating from the maddening noise and chaos is important for your peace of mind. Read the Bible or some other inspirational book. Indulge in a meditative activity such as closing your eyes and repeating an inspirational mantra, poem, or prayer.

Place a picture of your loved ones on your desk to remind you that work is just a small part of your life.

Hang some pictures in your office that represent what you are working for. They should depict something truly leisurely or inspirational.

Liven your office with some exotic plants. These will be a living reminder of nature and the importance of spending more time there.

Consider delegating upward on occasion. Let your boss do the work or make that important decision. Don't let your ego get in the way. On an important decision, just explain the problem and then ask your boss, "What would you do if you were in my position?"

On a regular basis, change the plants, paintings, pictures, and other positive objects in your office. Otherwise, you will become totally oblivious to them over the long term.

Make a point of having lunch with people who have nothing to do with your workplace. This should be a time for forgetting about your job rather than dwelling on it.

When you screw up at work, learn from your mistakes to make sure you don't make them again. But also learn to laugh at yourself and the absurdity of the situation.

At least once a year go through the whole work day pretending you are an alien from Mars and have just dropped to visit Earth. See how totally bizarre your workplace is.

When you experience anger or disappointment at work, take a short break to breathe deeply and relax. Reconnect with your essence and your spirituality.

If you hate your job and feel you can't quit, stop feeling sorry for yourself. Keep the words of Oscar Wilde in mind: "To toil for a master is bitter; but to have no master to toil for is more bitter still." Look at this job as a stepping stone to something better.

To prevent yourself from getting dissatisfied with your job, do everything within your power to make your job better. Look at all the positives of your job and try to turn around some of the negatives.

The Institute for Business Technology has declared the second Monday of February as Clean Out Your Computer Day. On this day organize your computer files and delete those not needed. Eliminating computer clutter will make you more efficient.

To create more time, be organized at work. At least once a month have a Clean Off Your Desk Day so that you can find things faster.

Create opportunities to revitalize yourself throughout the workday. Sneak ten minutes to read a comic book or inspirational book of quotations whenever possible.

While you're cleaning your desk, clean out your files and bookshelf as well. Like your messy closets at home, these can be a real drain of energy.

Give yourself permission to be more selective about reading or not reading what comes across your desk. Read only memos and reports that are relevant to your work and position.

Higher creativity will help you be more efficient and effective in all aspects of life, including your job. You can have many people wondering how you achieve more in a day than they do in two or three. After you have read *The Artist's Way* by Julia Cameron, spend even more time celebrating and developing your creativity. Read *A Whack on the Side of the Head* by Roger von Oech (Warner Books) or *The Joy of Thinking Big* by yours truly (Ten Speed Press).

Get the brainstorming card deck Thinkpak by creativity expert Michael Michalko (Ten Speed Press). This pack of fifty-six idea-stimulating cards can be used to create new ideas for how to be more efficient and productive in regular work hours.

In 1993, Rush Limbaugh declared that on January 12—his birthday—people should work harder. On Work Harder Day, show Rush Limbaugh that you are a peak performer by doing the opposite—work a little less and play more.

Whether you are self-employed or working for someone else, remind yourself that to be a peak performer, it's not the long hours or how hard you work that counts; it's how smart you work.

Put little reminders in your office about the need to have a more balanced life. On Post-it Notes write down all the things you will be missing out on if you work long hours.

Take work home with you only if your employer allows you to indulge in your favorite leisure activities at work.

If you take work home, do as little as possible because you won't be doing your best work there. Researchers at the University of Pittsburgh found that people's mental agility drops by as much as 30 percent at night.

If you have been at your job for a long time, look at it from a fresh perspective—as if you were just starting to work at this position.

When stress and tension strike, practice deep breathing to provide relief. Making a point to consciously breathe deeply and regularly throughout the day will make you more relaxed and energetic.

GORGEOUS MORNING, HUH DAD?

MM.

THESE SUMMER DAYS SURE SLIP BY, DON'T THEY? TOO BAD THE DAILY DRUDGERY OF MAKING A LIVING HAS TO KEEP YOU FROM APPRECIATING THESE SUBLIME MOMENTS OF LIFE.

WELL, BEST NOT TO THINK ABOUT IT.' IF YOU STAY HEALTHY, YOU CAN ENJOY DAYS LIKE THIS WHEN YOU RETIRE! SEE YOU TONIGHT!

AHHH. SUMMER!

Make a vacation out of your work. Invite your spouse (and kids if possible) to accompany you on one of your business trips.

Don't resist change; be open to it. It is a constant in today's workplace and even accelerating as time passes. Be confident about your ability to respond positively to change in the workplace.

It's relatively easy to be leisurely when you are away from the office. Ensure that you find the time to do something relaxing when you are the busiest at work, when you need it the most.

Embrace corporate absurdity. Try to find as much humor as you can in the inflated egos, personality conflicts, useless meetings, unattainable schedules, salary inequities, and mundane tasks your workplace has to offer.

Have a regular massage to relieve stress. If cost is an issue, check out community colleges with a massage program. Some give free massages as an opportunity for their students to polish their skills.

Smile more often at work to alleviate mental stress. Stanford University researchers found that frowning heats the brain while smiling cools it.

Author Michael A. Zigarelli advises Christians to bring their faith into the workplace by following Paul's admonition in Colossians: "Whatever you do, work at it with all your heart, as working for the Lord."

Stop leaving half-completed projects all around you. Concentrate on doing only one thing at a time, and you will end up completing a lot more things.

Keep idle chatter with coworkers to a minimum so that you get your work done and get out of the office at the regular quitting time.

**Throw away as much paperwork as you can.**

Don't be limited by your company's two- or three-week vacation policy. Take an extra week or two without pay to take an extended vacation.

Ask for what you want: shorter work hours, a more flexible schedule, or an extra few days off. You never can tell when your employer may give you exactly what you want.

Learn to recognize those time-consuming activities and tasks that don't need doing. Then make sure you don't do any of them.

Be careful what you wish for, because you may get it. If it's a promotion you want, keep in mind the words of Robert Frost: "By working faithfully eight hours a day, you may eventually get to be boss and work twelve hours a day."

If you feel that you deserve a raise for your unpaid overtime, then ask for it. Request an amount 10 to 20 percent higher than you think you are worth. If you get the raise, make sure that some of it goes toward a well-earned vacation.

Studies have shown that the last hour of the work day tends to be the least productive. Use this time for cleaning your desk, checking and sending e-mail, and other low-key activities

Given a chance to work less, do it! Remember that by giving up extra work and money, you gain more of a really precious commodity—time.

Work more to be than to acquire. It was Confucius who first said, "Choose a job you love, and you will never have to work a day in your life."

At the end of the work day change gears by shifting from the working mental state to the leisure mental state. If you can, walk home and use this time to wind down, or stop at the park for twenty minutes to relax. By the time you get home, you should have eliminated your thoughts about the workplace.

Never lose sight of the 80/20 principle: 80 percent of your production comes from 20 percent of your efforts. The remaining 20 percent of your production requires 80 percent of your time. To be more efficient, focus on the most lucrative areas of your work, and cut back on the less productive areas.

Move away from the office gossip, especially about co-workers. Productive and self-confident people don't have to indulge in this time-wasting activity.

Don't procrastinate by putting off the completion of a project when the end is near. Finish it without delay and go have some fun golfing, lovemaking, dancing, hiking, swimming, or dining.

Learn to say no. If you are efficient and productive, any decent boss will respect you for your unwillingness to have more work interfere with your personal life.

Don't allow phone calls at the end of the day to lengthen your work day. Ask the caller to call back in the morning.

Avoid trying to fit in just a little more work after official quitting time. This can lead to your working one to several hours of unpaid overtime and depriving your family and friends of your company.

# Daily Life

Put success in proper perspective. Success is not based on how much fame and fortune you acquire. Success is based on how much peace, satisfaction, health, and love you get to experience on this Earth.

In essays to the *Philadelphia Inquirer* many children revealed that they long for a traditional family dinner every night. No matter how busy your lifestyle, every day have at least one meal with your spouse and children—no excuses.

Whether or not you consider yourself artistically inclined, attempt something of an artistic nature. Take at least fifteen minutes a day to discover new talents. Create your own art or your own music or your own book.

Every sunset is different; so experience each one for its uniqueness.

After you have cut down on your TV watching, watch even less TV. Like many people, you may want to use the television to help wind down and relax. Unfortunately, research indicates it often has the opposite effect on viewers.

When you are stuck in a traffic jam, make the best of it. See if you can entertain those unhappy people in the cars around you. For example, write something funny in big letters on a piece of paper and share it with them.

It's not necessary for you to become involved in making small talk at a party just because it seems the polite thing to do. Go home promptly if the party is too boring and you have more interesting and enjoyable things to do.

Some managers and executives have a personal coach to motivate themselves to work harder and more efficiently. Instead, get together with a friend and the two of you can be leisure coaches for each other. Encourage one another to be more leisurely and enjoy life.

L earn to stop at STOP signs. Show the world that you are sufficiently mentally balanced to stop and care about safety for your family, yourself, and others.

R ead *Living, Loving & Learning* by Leo Buscaglia. If you have read it already, read it again.

**Indulge in a favorite weekly treat. You deserve it.**

T his weekend go somewhere new and interesting. Don't stick to your old haunts and hangouts. Wouldn't it be wild to escape to a place where you can rent a sailboat for the whole weekend? If this excites you, do it and send everyone you know a postcard!

Give some serious consideration to this bit of graffiti: "Hard work pays off in the future; Laziness pays off now!"

**Avoid seeing every situation as a challenge.**

Twice a year go to a restaurant where you can eat food you've never tried before.

Don't allow yourself to suffer from delusions of adequacy in regards to having a balanced lifestyle. If you hardly see or talk to your spouse, you suspect your kids could be on drugs, and you are stressed and miserable, you must start working on changing your lifestyle immediately!

Whenever you find yourself in a rush, tell yourself, "What's your hurry? Slow down and live!"

**Own more leisure clothes than formal ones.**

Show your spouse and kids that they have priority over your job. Let them plan a special outing at least once a month that requires that you leave the office on time.

Reach out to someone close to you everyday. Compliment them so that they feel good and it will make you feel good too.

When you have great neighbors, take the time to do a good deed for them. Remember that the smallest good deed far surpasses the best of intentions.

Are you having a tough day? Skim newspapers quickly looking only at the positive articles. However, take your time with the comics.

On a daily basis read a quotation from a book of inspirational quotations. A good source is *The Rubicon Dictionary of Positive, Motivational, Life-Affirming & Inspirational Quotations* compiled and arranged by John Cook.

To fight the blues develop a collection of jokes, articles, and cartoons that are really funny and make you laugh out loud. Totally immerse yourself in this collection when you feel down.

Philipa Walker offers some great advice: "Take time every day to do something silly."

Your kids like to know how special they are on a daily basis. Create the time to ensure your kids feel that they are needed, appreciated, and, most importantly, loved.

Take part in stimulating conversations more often for the cost of a coffee or a juice. All you have to do is find a cafe in your city that has a regular group meet to discuss politics, news events, or philosophy.

Limit the amount of television you and your children watch to one hour a day. The whole family will benefit. Some families have done away with their television set and report the quality of their family life increased.

Ever feel overstressed or down about life? Need a cure? Then take a brisk, long walk. Paul Dudley White stated, "A vigorous five-mile walk will do more good for an unhappy but otherwise healthy adult than all the medicine and psychology in the world."

Plan to watch at least one hour of TV less each day for the next year. This will give you 365 hours, or the equivalent of over fifteen 24-hour days to pursue more worthwhile leisure activities.

Negative thoughts tend to attract negative events. Positive thoughts tend to bring positive results. No matter what circumstances influence and dominate your life, you can always control how you react to them.

If you are making a good income—average or better—take this simple test: Do you have the time to enjoy your family and possessions? If you don't, establish a better balance before life flies right on by without you.

The key to an enjoyable vacation is not to put yourself under stress and duress. When on vacation, don't overschedule things to do. Allow for some spontaneity.

When going on vacation in your car, take your time. Add to your enjoyment by stopping to read the roadside signs about the historical points of interest.

To increase your vacation time, don't travel anywhere. Take a vacation at home and do some of those things you have always wanted to do.

When visiting a new place, check out the local cafés and diners instead of eating at the restaurants catering to the tourist trade. You will experience cheaper and better food as well as a more interesting atmosphere.

To make vacations more affordable, escape expensive hotels and meal costs by finding short-term apartments, villas, or cottage rentals. These can cost less than 50 percent of hotel room prices and be much more interesting to stay in.

Do the impossible: go on that trip you never thought was possible. If you don't have the money, start saving 2 percent of your income and you will have enough in a few years.

Cut down on expensive hotel rooms by exchanging houses with another family. Ask your travel agent for a list of organizations that will make the arrangements for a fee.

When on vacation, try going a whole week without your watch. Note how you are a slave to time by the number of times you are tempted to look at your wrist even though time is not that important.

Don't allow achievement to become an obsession. Take life as it comes and allow yourself to enjoy each and every situation as it presents itself. The more you enjoy yourself in these situations, the more you will achieve with minimal effort.

Alan Caruba, founder of the National Boring Institute, has declared July as National Anti-Boredom Month. Next July, make a point of doing everything within your power to avoid boredom because it can cause depression, addictions, and other serious afflictions. Use everything you learn about avoiding boredom for the rest of the year.

When thinking about retirement, consider that health and fitness are the two most important ingredients for successful retirement. For both a healthy mind and a healthy body—use it or lose it!

Our highest expectations are responsible for our biggest disappointments. Take a more Buddhist approach to life: expect nothing and appreciate everything that flows your way.

Most kids would rather spend time in a dentist's chair than go to music lessons. Don't spend time trying to send your kids to music lessons if they don't want to go. Why waste their time and yours?

**Save time by shopping via catalogs.**

Ensure that your kids do their share of chores around the house so that you don't have to use your time and energy to account for their neglect. Don't clean up your children's mess; that's their responsibility.

Go one step further. Be creative in getting your kids to do more than their share of chores so that you end up with more free time on your hands.

Don't tell your children how to do their chores. Just tell them what must be done. They may show you how to get those chores done creatively in a new and faster way.

To ease the pressure for you to work so hard to support your family, encourage your kids to have part-time jobs. They will benefit, too, from developing good work habits and being able to purchase some of the things they want themselves.

**Send cards and flowers to your mate for no apparent reason.**

Show your respect and love for your children by attending all the sports contests, school plays, and other events in which they get involved.

Share meal preparation. Make it your turn on even days and your partner's turn on odd days.

At least twice a year, to have more time for romance or time with the rest of your family, splurge to employ the services of a caterer to prepare dinner at your home.

If you can't nap at work, make a point of taking a nap every Saturday and Sunday afternoon.

Quit collecting things for the sake of acquisition. Do you really need more than one set of dishes, towels, bedding, kitchen utensils, or car tools?

If you catch yourself arguing with a friend or relative, ask yourself where the argument may lead. What is the payoff? Why not offer to buy the person with whom you are arguing a drink or a cup of coffee and talk about something else?

Quit speeding in your car. Slow down even if you are in a hurry. Drive as you would like everyone else to drive when your children are in the area.

Eileen Buchheim of *Celebrate Romance* has declared February as Creative Romance Month. Have an affair with your spouse. Take the initiative and do many things wild and passionate throughout the month.

Develop friendships with people with whom you can share your negative experiences that come with having a bad day. Share your concerns so that you don't end up internalizing them. Be careful, though, that you aren't always sharing negative thoughts with your friends.

Don't insist on doing everything alone. Overcome your ego and ask for assistance.

When traveling, be an explorer and not a tourist. Look for quality and not quantity. Spend a week or two in one place to really get to know the people, the lifestyles, and the customs of that particular part of the country.

**Travel lightly wherever you go. Pack only what you need.**

Designate at least one night a week as family night. Everyone has to be at home by 6:00 P.M. and stay in for the entire evening. Allow no visitors and use the answering machine to intercept calls. Play games, rent a movie, or tell each other stories.

Learn to say no more often; say it quickly and firmly. If the person persists, don't get involved in a verbal battle. Just say no again. Real friends and reasonable acquaintances will respect your need for more time for yourself.

Morton C. Orman of the Health Resources Network has declared April 16 as National Stress Awareness Day. Take a break on the day after income taxes are due.

**At least once in your life plant a tree. Hug one, too.**

Review the good times you have had in your life by going through your photo albums. Choose one or two things you have enjoyed in the past and do them again.

Life will throw many curve balls your way. When it does, laugh at whatever you can. A humorous perspective will help you lighten up and get over the tough going a lot sooner.

Accept that in large measure living a rewarding life is a state of mind. It's not what you do for a living and how hard you work that count. What counts is the attitude that you display at work and play.

Take an extended vacation with Earthwatch and learn many interesting things at the same time. Earthwatch can put you on projects such as helping scientists count whales off the coast of Australia or assisting archaeologists excavate ancient settlements in Russia, the Pacific Spice Islands, or Easter Island.

Avoid wasting your time and someone else's when asked for information you don't have. Be gratified to answer promptly; say you don't know.

Buy the most relaxing chairs and sofas that you can find and not the most esthetic.

To enhance your family's leisure time and quality of life, take part in National TV Turn-Off Week during the last week of April.

Be adventurous with the food you eat. Here's a partial list of the different types of restaurants to visit and enjoy: Chinese, Thai, Japanese, Vegetarian, Ukrainian, Greek, Spanish, Italian, Mexican, German, Cajon, Vietnamese, and Malaysian.

Go to a big supermarket, and purchase the vegetables and fruits you have never eaten. When you get home, prepare a meal with them.

Make a point of smiling ten times a day or more. Studies show that smiling involves facial muscles that send signals to the brain causing your emotional state to improve.

Have frequent spontaneous celebrations that acknowledge small but significant leisure accomplishments, such as finishing a painting, completing a course, catching a fish, or meeting new neighbors.

Be less competitive. Fully functioning individuals don't think of life as a competition with everyone else.

Avoid restaurants with an attitude. Dine where the customers and employees are having the best time. The contagious enthusiasm will benefit you. You should be energized by the restaurant and not demoralized.

Don't waste your time blowing your horn at someone leaving a parking spot. Pennsylvania researchers found that the average driver will take twenty-six seconds to back out of a parking spot when no one is waiting, thirty-one seconds when another car is waiting for the spot, and forty-three seconds when the driver of the waiting car honks the horn to get the driver to hurry.

When undertaking new life challenges, be oblivious to your age and watch your stress level go down.

Hang around wise people. You will learn a lot in a short period of time.

∞

Once a year make contact with an old friend or colleague you haven't talked to for at least three years to find out how he or she is doing.

∞

Attend functions where people are interested in something you have never been interested in. Ask a lot of questions. You will learn a lot more than at functions where everyone has the same interests as you.

The composer Rossini worked in bed and according to some rumors was so lazy that if he dropped a sheet of music, he'd rewrite the whole page rather than get out of bed and pick it up. On that note, take the time regularly to be lazy and be proud of it.

Adopt the philosophy of Rita Mae Brown: "I finally figured out the only reason to be alive is to enjoy it."

At least once in your life, use a tactic from Peter Hansen, the author of *The Joy of Stress*. When he was writing his book, instead of driving to work, he hired a limousine so he could relax and be less stressed when he arrived at the office and home.

Statistics provide overwhelming evidence that you are going to die. It could be sooner than later. Start doing those important things in life as soon as possible because you may not get as many chances as you are hoping for.

Don't allow advertisers and others to influence you into thinking you have to celebrate Thanksgiving in a commercialized way. You don't have to cook big dinners and entertain others if you don't feel like it.

Stop wasting time and energy trying to solve other people's problems. People will solve their own problems on their own when they are ready. In addition, your trying to solve their problems is tantamount to saying they aren't capable of doing it on their own.

Don't force yourself to try and sleep eight hours a day when you can get by with seven or less. Many people worry about not being able to sleep eight hours when in fact they don't need it. About one in five adults is a short sleeper who needs six hours or less of sleep.

When you can't sleep, continuing to lie in bed won't help. Get up and do something satisfying.

Take a yoga class to find out how you can use this ancient art to increase your energy, improve breathing, tone muscles, and reduce stress.

An unknown wise person said, "Doing the same thing over and over, expecting different results, is the definition of crazy." If you are not getting satisfaction in your life, then rearrange it.

Mark Twain said, "When you cannot get a compliment in any other way, pay yourself one." Even if you receive many compliments from others, give yourself at least one compliment every day.

Once a month celebrate your contribution to this world. Don't underrate your achievements. Make a list of all the good things you have done in the last month.

Make sure that your telephone is there to serve you instead of serving everyone else. Use your answering machine or a call monitoring display to ensure that you are talking to only those people who you want to talk to.

When you clean your house, don't just move your stuff from one place to another. Sort through it and be honest with yourself as to whether you need it around. Throw out, give away, or recycle as much as you can.

A void associating with people who are always late. They are not showing respect for you and are making you waste precious time waiting for them.

∞

T ake time to smell the roses . . . and the tulips . . . . and the daffodils . . . . and the violets . . . . . and the . . . .

∞

**Don't just smell the flowers; plant some as well.**

∞

B e more of a participant and less of a spectator. Instead of going to games or watching them on TV, spend time playing these sports.

Buy a case of champagne. Designate each of the twelve bottles for a special day to celebrate over the next six months.

For a healthier you, try to spend at least thirty minutes outside each day. Studies show that there are twenty to thirty times as many pollutants in the average house as outside.

Take up a new sport or other activity just for the fun of it. No other reason! You will find it's quite exhilarating to try something you have been thinking about doing for years.

On the third Monday of every year, celebrate Oprah Winfrey's holiday. In 1994, she named this day National Thank You Day to thank everyone who has helped her out.

Lily Tomlin offers some wise words of advice: "For fast relief, try slowing down."

Turn off the television and radio when having dinner with someone else.

To show your appreciation for your fortune in life, often do something kind for someone less fortunate than you.

If you must criticize and complain, then spend four times as much time praising and expressing gratitude as you do criticizing and complaining. This is the way it should be—studies show that 80 percent of the events in our lives are positive and 20 percent are negative.

Go to the library with no specific book or topic in mind. Allow the interesting books to discover you.

When you are in a hurry in city traffic, show some courtesy and generosity by allowing people to pull their cars in front of yours. What goes around comes around.

Invite someone new to your home. Share your photographs, art, scrapbook, old love letters, musical instrument, and favorite CDs.

Watch videos of *Monty Python, Candid Camera, Laurel and Hardy,* and *The Three Stooges.* A night of comedy will help you forget your woes.

Your brain needs exercise just like the rest of your body. Use it or lose it as you age. To keep it sharp, buy books of brain teasers and do all of them.

Refuse to be a slave to tradition. Preserve tradition only if there is some enjoyment and satisfaction in the activity. Otherwise, the heck with tradition

Avoid overloading your brain with excessive multi-tasking. Trying to do too many things at the same time—cooking on the stove, washing clothes, watching TV, talking on the cell phone, and printing documents on the computer—will prevent you from thinking clearly. Taking on too much will also leave you feeling overwhelmed and stressed out.

Beware of technology interfering with your relationships. You can end up insulating yourself from members of your family by working on the computer or playing video games for hours.

If you declare that you are committed to your children's well-being, show it. One research study found adults in the United States spend an average of six hours each week in shopping malls compared to about forty-five minutes of quality time with their children.

On a rainy day open the windows and take a nap on the sofa. A nap with the sound of the rain falling can be a most pleasurable and relaxing experience.

Make the small pleasures in life your biggest priorities. Oscar Wilde stated, "I adore simple pleasures. They are the last refuge of the complex."

When traveling between major cities on the U.S. West Coast, opt for a bus ride from Green Tortoise of San Francisco. These low-cost trips are for the adventurous who can enjoy a lack of exact itineraries and guaranteed arrival times and instead experience vegetarian cookouts and unscheduled stops at hot springs.

Save time packing for a vacation by making a list of travel necessities and keeping it in your suitcase for future trips.

If you get bored mowing the lawn, try being artistic. Make a different interesting pattern every time you cut the grass.

At least once a month go to lunch with someone who has an incredible zest for life.

Thank God that all your wants and needs have not been answered. Saint Theresa of Avila offered some food for thought: "More tears are shed over answered prayers than unanswered ones."

Help others slow down and find time to really live. We teach best what we most have to learn ourselves.

The Hindus have a powerful proverb: "You grow only when you are alone." Even if you are married, create the time to spend an hour or two each day alone. This is your special time for creative solitude to paint, read, write, or meditate away from others.

Spending time judging life's events can be unproductive and a drain of energy. Most of our troubles come from how we interpret, label, and judge the events that shape our lives. Tame your voice of judgment by paying attention to your mind's constant evaluation based on right-wrong, good-bad, and black-white.

If you don't have the cash, get an additional mortgage of $10,000 on your house and go to India with your spouse for three weeks. A friend of mine and his wife—both in their early fifties—did just this. Not knowing whether they would be healthy enough to do this later, they decided to do it now.

If Christmas is a big source of stress due to the shopping for gifts, cooking big meals, and spending time with dysfunctional relatives, change your ways and do something less traditional. Who says you have to do what the majority in society do?

Even if you enjoy traditional Christmas celebrations, add variety to your life by doing something different next Christmas. Go to Fiji or the Cayman Islands and experience how people there celebrate Christmas.

Be really clear that on Mother's Day it is more important to give the gift of your time than flowers and other presents. Did you know that the woman who was instrumental in having the U.S. government declare Mother's Day spent the rest of her money and life fighting the commercialization of this holiday?

When the leaves fall off the trees in autumn, make sure you enjoy their beauty before you rake and bag them. Smell them. Look at them. Listen to them. Touch them. Even taste them.

Pay attention to these suggestions from a group of people all over sixty years old who were asked what advice they would give themselves if they had life to live over:

- Don't get married until you are ready to take responsibility.

- Take the time to find what you really want to do with your life.

- Take more risks.

- Lighten up! Don't take life so seriously.

- Be more patient.

- Live the moment more.

Your past will always be a reflection of the way things really were. Stop wasting time trying to change it.

Energize yourself right now: go for a bicycle ride. Read the rest of this book later.

You may have settled into a vacation routine that is too comfortable and predictable. Have your kids plan the next vacation.

When in between jobs, take a vacation for a month or two. Make your goal to be as leisurely as possible.

Make a list of all the important things money can't buy. Are you ensuring that you are doing everything within your power to put these things in your life today?

Choose new friends wisely. Look at their character and personality instead of what they do for a living or how much money or social status they have. Those who don't expect anything from you are also a good bet. It is better to form a few deep, close friendships instead of many superficial ones.

Reject society's judgment of your role in this world and how hard you must work to be a decent person. If you can make a good living by working two hours a day, do it!

Try to go through the whole day smiling at people and the world around you. Remember that you require seventy-two of your muscles to frown and only fourteen to smile.

Paint a picture at least once a year with the words of Clement Greenberg in mind: "All profoundly original art looks ugly at first." If you think your painting looks like the bottom of Lake Superior, don't worry about it. Share the painting with your friends anyway.

On the way home from work buy your lover a present for no reason at all. When you get home, celebrate even more with a good bottle of wine.

Take a stroll down a familiar street but this time carefully observe everything you can. You will be amazed how many interesting things you have never noticed before.

Do something nice for someone regardless of how good or bad you feel. Being a good Samaritan will have a positive effect on your well-being.

You don't have to take part in certain family events just because your relatives are going to be there. If certain relatives cause you more stress and disruption than it's worth, spend your time with friends or alone.

Ultimately the quality of our lives depends on how much we are willing to put into them. If satisfaction is missing from your life, answer this: Who is the one person who can make your life more satisfying?

**Have a heart-to-heart conversation with a six-year-old. You'll be reminded of what really matters.**

Say nice things about special people in your life when they aren't around. Say even nicer things about special people in your life when they are around.

Climb a tree and see the world from a different perspective.

Ask yourself at the end of each day, "What have I done today to make my life more complete?"

At least twice a year indulge in a special treat that takes you away from your normal environment. For example, spend a few days at a spa or retreat for total relaxation.

Wake up each morning with leisure activities having as much importance as work. Put as much time into planning your leisure as you do in planning your work.

Keep in mind the Italian proverb "A happy heart is better than a full purse."

When your voice of judgment tells you that you shouldn't go out and enjoy yourself because this would be frivolous or nonproductive, do the opposite. Have at least one day a week during which you can be impractical.

Most people celebrate life only when things are going great or some special thing occurs. It's more important to celebrate life to the fullest when things aren't going so well. Leo Buscaglia, author of *Living, Loving, and Learning,* talks about how his wonderful mother surprised the family with a big feast the day after his father had lost all the money in some wacky business deal. "This is when we need it the most," she explained

Pay heed to the words of Andy Rooney: "Learn to enjoy the little things in life because the big ones don't come around often."

Stop and talk to homeless street people. Find out what makes them tick. Ask what is truly interesting and important to them. You'll may get a new positive perspective on life.

An old Chinese proverb states, "My house burnt down, but now I can see the moon." If you are prepared to look for it, there is a silver lining in practically every cloud, no matter how dark the cloud.

Call forth the best you can muster for living life to the fullest no matter how limited your income or funds. The Greeks have an important inspirational saying: "When you are poor, it is important to have a good time."

According to Samuel Johnson, most people spend parts of their lives in attempts to display qualities they don't have. If you are one of these people, stop wasting your time and energy! Anyone worth knowing will discover your true qualities sooner or later.

Waste little time fantasizing or worrying about the future. It'll be here soon enough. People who spend quality time in the present find that the future takes care of itself.

Read at least five good books a year. This is no time to speed read. Keep the words of Thomas Babington Macaulay in mind: "A page slowly digested is better than a volume hurriedly read."

Don't be so worried that if you let it all hang out, then you will have made a total fool of yourself and you won't be able to go out in public again. This is nonsense. You have done this before and you have done quite well.

Make a point of learning something new every day. A Latin proverb states, "A learned man has riches within himself." No matter how old you are, there's always something interesting to learn.

To help you enjoy the moment for what it is and to be in the here and now, have your clock or watch alarm go off at various times during the day. Use this as a reminder to have the presence of mind to get totally immersed in what you are doing, no matter what it is.

Do your part to help out at school, church, or community events. It doesn't cost anything and is a great way to socialize and eat some great food.

Give due consideration to these wise words of George Bernard Shaw: "A day's work is a day's work, neither more nor less, and the man who does it needs a day's sustenance, a night's repose and due leisure, whether he be painter or ploughman."

Walk the talk. Even though 91 percent of Americans agreed that "the buy-now, pay-later attitude causes many of us to consume more than we need," few do anything to reverse this. If you agree with this statement, it's time for you to show some integrity by cutting down on your consumption.

Even if you don't like cooking, learn how to make at least three great dishes. Share these with others when they visit.

Confucius gave this advice: "To be wronged is nothing unless you continue to remember it." Learn to forgive people who have done you wrong. When you refuse to forgive, you haven't imprisoned the other person; you have imprisoned yourself.

You won't have to carry a grudge if you start believing in this French proverb: "The best revenge is to live well."

Truly experience an apple or an orange before eating it. Look at it very carefully. Dissect it and study the texture of the inside and the outside. Smell it. Touch it. Listen to it. Bite into it, slowly. Savor each bite.

**Throw surprise parties for people who matter in your life.**

Remember that a satisfying life is not determined so much by how long we live as by how well we live. Some people die at forty-five but they have squeezed in a heck of a lot more real living in those forty-five years than others who have lived to be ninety or a hundred.

Studies show that 40 percent of our worries are about events that will never happen, 30 percent of our worries are about events that already happened, 22 percent of our worries are about trivial events, 4 percent of our worries are about real events we cannot change, and only 4 percent of our worries are about real events on which we can act. This means that 96 percent of the things we worry about are things we can't control. This signifies 96 percent of our worrying is wasted.

In fact, it is even worse than that. Worrying about things we can control is also useless, since we can control these things. In other words, worrying about things we can't control is wasted because we can't control them, and worrying about things we can control is wasted because we can control them. The result is 100 percent of our worrying is wasted.

Take a lesson from the people on the island of Crete, who have a low rate of heart disease. Researchers feel the reason is they get plenty of physical exercise, use monounsaturated olive oil to cook, and eat lots of fish, fresh fruits and vegetables, and relatively little red meat.

Don't stop just to smell the flowers. Stop and smell the various coffee beans the next time you are in a gourmet coffeehouse.

Learn how to live one day at a time and you will have learned the secret of how to live happily ever after.

Twice a month go to the library for an hour or two and research topics you don't know anything about. Learning throughout life will give you a sense of well-being, help you think better, and enhance your longevity.

You must deal with the attendant emotions if you are the nice person who tries to help everyone you know. Instead of being a nice person, be a good person who helps only those who need or deserve it.

Don't take your health for granted. Good health is often not appreciated until it's lost—sometimes for good. Consciously do at least three things every day that enhance your health.

Get rid of telephone solicitors quickly so that they don't rob you of precious time. Here are a few lines you can use when you get one on your telephone:

⚮ "I will only talk to you if you tell me a really dirty joke."

⚮ "I only buy things from people who have first bought what I sell—and I sell Ferraris."

⚮ "First, you have to tell me the brand and color of your underwear."

⚮ "Can you call back in about ten minutes? I am just completing my application for welfare."

⚮ "Yes, my spouse is at home, but I never let her (him) talk to strangers."

⚮ "You want to sell me insurance. Great, I have been trying to buy insurance for years but nobody will ever sell me any."

⚮ "Guess what? I can play 'Mary Had A Little Lamb' on the telephone." Then play it on the touch-tone phone: 6-5-4-5 666, 555, 666.

In the midst of a turbulent week, take an hour or two to experience total solitude and silence. Don't talk to anyone. Shut off the phones, don't look at e-mail, don't watch TV, don't listen to the radio, and don't answer the door.

Don't be like the corporate fast-trackers who engage in their leisure with as much, or more, competitiveness than in their work. Make sure most of your leisure activities are noncompetitive.

List all the things you would like to experience if you had the extra time. Then write down all the excuses you can muster for not doing them. Finally, sit down with a friend and shoot holes through all the excuses.

Go back to the list of special things you have always wanted to experience. Make up three reasons why you can do them in the next year. Then do them.

Never be too busy to see high-class acts, such as the Rolling Stones, Celine Dion, Garth Brooks, Bryan Adams, Alanis Morissette, or Luciano Pavarotti, when they visit your city.

If you have a healthy balance between work and play, refuse to alter your leisurely behavior for anyone. Remember these words of an unknown wise person: "How many people do you know who on their deathbed said, 'I wish I would have worked more.'?"

Risk more at your leisure. Don't be afraid to play tennis or golf with someone who is much better than you. You'll learn a lot and get better at the game quicker.

**Avoid the extreme behaviors of indulgence or deprivation. Make it a rule to practice moderation in everything you undertake.**

It's not necessary to reciprocate out of a sense of obligation when someone has had you over for dinner. If you don't feel like having the people over, don't. You have already done your part by going to their place when they invited you and you accepted.

Occasionally break the prior rule of moderation. Overdo one of your favorite leisure activities. Do you like walking in the park? Go for two hours instead of your normal half-hour.

Once in a while do something beneficial for someone you don't know who will never find out.

Don't neglect the spiritual self. People who have a deep and rich inner life are best able to deal with the trials and tribulations of the outside world.

Borrow an idea from Oprah Winfrey: keep a gratitude journal. At the end of every day count your blessings, and write down at least five wonderful things that happened to you.

Learn to laugh at yourself. Imitate Rodney Dangerfield, Steven Wright, or Joan Rivers by making up one-liners about your terrible situation in life.

Get a variety of twenty magazines that you or someone else is ready to throw away or recycle. Cut out all the pictures, images, and cartoons to make a collage that reflects what you like about life and dreams.

Are you stuck in a rut—at work or play? The only difference between a rut and a grave are the dimensions. Do everything you can to get out of your rut. Reinvent your life.

Be clear on how wealth stacks up against life's other pleasures. Ted Turner said, "Average sex is better than being a billionaire."

Break some of the written and unwritten rules society has laid out for us. It was Katherine Hepburn who said, "If you obey all the rules, you miss all the fun."

When you don't have enough time for your hour of exercise, at least spend fifteen or thirty minutes. You will feel a lot better than if you don't do any.

Assume that on your deathbed you beg God, "Please give me one more shot, and I will give it all I've got." God replies that you can have one more year. Make a list of what you would do in that year before you die and carry it with you at all times. Make a commitment to do all those things within the next year or two.

If you like parties and haven't gone to one for a while, throw one yourself. Have a wine-tasting party or a theme party.

Try being a panhandler for half a day to experience a totally different way of life. To be more entrepreneurial at this, add a new twist—offer to tell jokes for a dollar or two.

Learn to distinguish those battles that are worth fighting and those that are not. There will be times when you are laboring at something that just won't work out the way you expected. It's never too late to scrap the project and start a new and more promising one.

Make the quality of your life job number one. If you always feel rushed, reduce the quantity of activities so that you get more quality in those you pursue.

Be decisive—especially about the small things—knowing that sometimes you are going to be wrong.

Most leisure activities that involve nature cost little or no money. Listen for all of the interesting sounds. Pay attention to the things bright and beautiful. Try star-gazing, bird-watching, and sailing.

Energize yourself. Clean your cupboards and refrigerator of all unhealthy foods. Load up on fresh fruit and vegetables.

Research at the University of Southern California confirms that variety *is* the spice of life. People with many interests live not only longest but happiest, too. Constantly challenge your inhibitions about trying new activities or going to new and different places.

Have more than one purpose in life. In fact, have many irons in the fire. Look toward new books to read, different people to meet, and vacation spots to visit.

**Don't ever postpone making love to do work of any kind.**

Develop a new appreciation for the things you take for granted, such as the fresh smell of coffee, a gentle wind blowing in your face, and the purring of your cat.

Every morning ask yourself, "How's my attitude today?" If it isn't great, give yourself an attitude change. Alter your attitude and you will alter your life.

Be a perpetual optimist. Replace anger, fear, and guilt with love, joy, and peace. Studies show optimistic people are healthier and live longer. Wake up every morning and decide to be as happy as anybody can be all day.

Don't allow your mind to play tricks on you by convincing you that you don't have time to spend with the kids or to pursue a new leisure activity. Assuming that you sleep seven hours every day, you have 1,020 minutes to spend while awake. Certainly, you can find thirty or sixty or even ninety minutes out of those 1,020 to be more leisurely.

If you're in the rat race, ask yourself why? There is no prize for outrunning a rat. No one is forcing you to lead a hurried life; you are the one who has chosen it.

Every day reach out and touch someone with a handshake, touch, or a hug.

When problems arise, perform some mental magic using your creativity. Look at old problems from new angles, and chances are you will come up with a new blockbuster solution or an obvious one that has been staring you in the face all along.

Especially when you are doing something difficult, tedious, or extremely time-consuming, ask yourself what would happen if you didn't do it. If the answer is nothing, or next to nothing, stop doing it.

Allow more chance in your life. The more chance you let in your world, the more interesting your world will become.

Don't miss the moment; master it. If you postpone the chance to live life, it may slip away altogether. The time to live is now.

You must be accountable for your boredom. Confront it when it strikes. Your willingness to take responsibility for your boredom is the creative force that will eliminate it.

The Academy of Leisure Sciences have determined that we get the most satisfaction from leisure activities that are harder and more challenging than passive activities such as watching TV or playing bingo. Put your time into activities requiring high levels of physical and intellectual energy.

You don't always need a reason for everything you do. For example, have dinner at midnight with no reasonable explanation to account for your actions.

Respect all types of lifestyles. Adopt one far different from yours for a month or two.

**Never be too busy to say** *please, thank you,* **or** *you're welcome.*

Avoid trouble any time you can. It's a lot easier to avoid trouble than it is to get out of it.

Dream big about taking a long vacation or a sabbatical. Put a little money away each month and in time you will get to enjoy your dream.

When you think you have simplified your life enough, simplify even more. Clutter adds to stress. Throw out your surplus magazines, clothes, and other items if you haven't used them in the last six months.

Zen it. Try to enjoy whatever you are doing no matter how tedious it may seem. Surrender to what you are doing when you begin doing it. Keep in mind that you have chosen the task and can always choose not to do it.

Accept that truly successful people show a concern for the world around them. Their focus is not just on themselves and their career or business but also on the environment, the poor, the disadvantaged, and the need for world peace.

Be spontaneous on a regular basis. Every day do something you haven't planned. It can be quite a small thing like taking a different route somewhere, eating in a different restaurant, or going to some new kind of entertainment.

**Adopt the slogan "To work is human, to loaf divine."**

Much happiness is lost in the pursuit of it. Allow yourself to react happily to things as they happen instead of trying to force happy things to happen. Stop trying so hard to be happy and watch the good times roll.

Risk and be more adventurous in your work and play. If your path in life feels really safe, then it probably is not the right path.

Find reasons to do the important things, instead of reasons not to do them. Risk, experiment, and don't forget to have some fun while you are at it.

Accept that if you have been looking for happiness and haven't found it, you have been looking in the wrong places. Happiness is where you find it. It can be a long way away or it can be where you are now, staring you in the face.

Several times a week relax by not doing anything in particular for an hour or two. Author Scott Peck, who has a full and busy life, is often asked, "How can you do all that you do?" His normal reply is, "Because I spend at least two hours a day doing nothing."

Don't spend a lot of time judging people. You have more valuable things to do with your life. Besides, that's God's job.

Be a maître d' to the good life by spreading joy wherever you are. Try to live like you are the greatest lover of life this universe has ever seen. Do this for a week or a month and watch your life change.

Of three precious resources in life—time, money, and creativity—the only one unlimited is your creativity. Make creativity your number one resource, and time and money won't be as precious.

Also from Prima

## A Five-Step Program to Turn Your Dreams into Reality!

Making dreams come true is everyone's fantasy. You know you need to set a goal, but how do you do it? Once you've defined a goal for yourself, how do you achieve it? And what can you do about obstacles that stand in your way? Here, bestselling author Don Gabor presents an easy-to-follow, five-step process that will help you realize your most ambitious personal and professional goals. Inside, you will discover how to:

- Make a commitment
- Identify your obstacles
- Overcome the fear of failure
- Activate your plans
- And much more!

ISBN 0-7615-0535-0
Paperback / 304 pages
U.S. $15.00 / Can. $22.00

PRIMA

**To order, call (800) 632-8676 or
visit us online at www.primalifestyles.com**

# Let the Wisdom of the Ages Guide You to a Richer, Fuller Life

Life is a series of profound events through which we all pass—leaving home, discovering a soul mate, raising a family, changing careers, growing older. The way in which we approach these and other passages determines the richness of our lives. In this book, you'll find timeless wisdom to guide and inspire you to embrace these events and achieve a fuller life. Author Nadine Crenshaw has woven together life-enhancing reflections from such ancient and contemporary minds as Shakespeare, Virginia Woolf, Voltaire, Eleanor Roosevelt, Robert Browning, and others.

ISBN 0-7615-1236-5
Paper over board / 224 pages
U.S. $18.00 / Can. $26.50

**To order, call (800) 632-8676 or visit us online at www.primalifestyles.com**

# Order Books

Please send me the following items:

| Quantity | Title | Unit Price | Total |
|---|---|---|---|
| _____ | <u>Big Things Happen When You</u> | _____ | $ _____ |
| _____ | <u>Do the Little Things Right</u> | $ 15.00 | $ _____ |
| _____ | <u>The Art of Living</u> | $ 18.00 | $ _____ |

|  |  |
|---|---|
| Subtotal | $ _____ |
| Deduct 10% when ordering 3–5 books | $ _____ |
| 7.25% Sales Tax (CA only) | $ _____ |
| 8.25% Sales Tax (TN only) | $ _____ |
| 5% Sales Tax (MD and IN only) | _____ |
| 7% G.S.T. Tax (Canada only) | $ _____ |
| Shipping and Handling* | $ _____ |
| Total Order | $ _____ |

*Shipping and Handling depend on Subtotal.

| Subtotal | Shipping/Handling |
|---|---|
| $0.00–$29.99 | $4.00 |
| $30.00–$49.99 | $6.00 |
| $50.00–$99.99 | $10.00 |
| $100.00–$199.99 | $13.50 |
| $200.00+ | Call for Quote |

Foreign and all Priority Request orders:
Call Customer Service
for price quote at 916-632-4400

This chart represents the total retail price of books only (before applicable discounts are taken).

**By Telephone:** With MC, Visa, or American Express, call 800-632-8676 or 916-632-4400.
Mon–Fri, 8:30-4:30.

**WWW:** http://www.primapublishing.com

**By Internet E-mail:** sales@primapub.com

**By Mail:** Just fill out the information below and send with your remittance to:

**Prima Publishing ▪ P.O. Box 1260BK ▪ Rocklin, CA 95677**

Name _____

Address_____

City _____ State _____ ZIP_____

MC/Visa/American Express# _____ Exp. _____

Check/money order enclosed for $_____ Payable to Prima Publishing

Daytime telephone _____

Signature _____